About the Author

Lauren Sheetz is a poet, creative, and speech-language pathologist who is emerging into the book world for the first time. She was born in Connecticut, with a passion for writing at a young age. We see her first published content in the poetry book *Phoenix*, where she specializes in short, powerful excerpts covering pieces of her journey. Lauren moved to Florida in 2020 to embark on a solo journey while using writing as a creative outlet. She is known to have a phoenix tattoo covering the majority of her back, which has inspired the title for her first book.

Phoenix

Lauren Sheetz

Phoenix

Olympia Publishers
London

www.olympiapublishers.com
OLYMPIA PAPERBACK EDITION

Copyright © Lauren Sheetz 2024

The right of Lauren Sheetz to be identified as author of
this work has been asserted in accordance with sections 77 and 78 of
the Copyright, Designs and Patents Act 1988.

All Rights Reserved

No reproduction, copy or transmission of this publication
may be made without written permission.
No paragraph of this publication may be reproduced,
copied or transmitted save with the written permission of the publisher,
or in accordance with the provisions
of the Copyright Act 1956 (as amended).

Any person who commits any unauthorized act in relation to
this publication may be liable to criminal
prosecution and civil claims for damage.

A CIP catalogue record for this title is
available from the British Library.

ISBN: 978-1-80439-752-7

This is a work of fiction.
Names, characters, places and incidents originate from the writer's
imagination. Any resemblance to actual persons, living or dead, is
purely coincidental.

First Published in 2024

Olympia Publishers
Tallis House
2 Tallis Street
London
EC4Y 0AB

Printed in Great Britain

Dedication

I dedicate *Phoenix* to my past, present, and future self – you are loved in every form.

Acknowledgments

Thank you to my sisters, Brianna and Julia, for encouraging me to always follow my dreams. My first best friends in this wonderful life. I am so grateful for your support and to live life alongside you. Thank you to my parents – Lucy, Bill, and Teresa – for providing stability, love, and support when needed most. Those core values never go unnoticed and I would be nowhere without you. Thank you to Leila and PJ for simply being constant lights in my life. Your existence alone brings me joy. And thank you to Olympia Publishers for believing in my work and taking the chance on my first book. I will be forever grateful that you helped create my first dream in physical form.

Part 1: Fall 2018

one warm
mid-April day
my sister asked me
what my biggest fear was

I said change

when I opened
my acceptance letter
to the next two years of my life
it felt like a ton of bricks buried me deep
into the ground

my lungs lost all airflow

I knew graduate school
was the expected next step
but I didn't expect my life
to backtrack ten steps

whose dream am I fulfilling?
because mine
is still hiding in my third-grade notebook
waiting for me to set it free

anxiety
is the worst bug I ever caught

a lingering restlessness
indulging in my system
feasting on me like a leech

how do I silence it

my heart began to flutter fast
and my fingers twitched
as if high from a sugar rush

nothing was calm any more

thirty-nine brilliant brains
sat surrounding me
it was sharply intimidating

– graduate school

maybe this is exactly what I needed:
a distraction from afflicting affairs

I told myself it was
the perfect time to forget you

I would bury my nose into my books
instead of beneath your waistline

the only place I want to be
is nestled between your arms

but nestled between your arms
is the only place I never am

my mind spins wild
at the sound of your name
simply that thread of letters
drives my body insane

you turn my insides into gold
melt me down deep
kiss the chill from my bones
you defrost me

your tongue whispered words
that brought goosebumps
they hit my spine so divine
then moved across me like poetry

how am I supposed
to reject something
that is so good
it makes my cheeks hot
and my knees weak

you have a way with words
that tongue
that tone
is explicitly delicious

a distinct difference lies
between being wanted and being cared for
I played with the ideas of both
wondering which box was mine
as if I didn't always know
it was the first one

you charm me
in the best way but steal my soul so selfishly

you
are the definition of toxicity
you need to drain from my veins
like the rain pipes
after a summer storm

think marathon legs:
constantly putting in work
never giving up despite the pain
despite the deterioration happening inside them
moving against others who want it too
it's always a competition
that's what you do to me

I'm not as naive as you think

I knew it was never just you and I

your heart loved company too much

I told myself it was okay to still see you
since I knew what I signed up for
it would hurt less if I expected the pain
how foolish of me to believe that

swirling in circles
under the dim orange light
I control your soul like a genie
fixated on my hips
the sweet smell of cigar smoke lingers on your lips
as you move glossy eyes in a slowed rotation
burning through the ashy Dutch
hiding beneath a cloud of lust
as those eyes linger lowly fueling with desire
I give you what you want not what I need
and choke back chalky pain
as my hips elevate and descend in a vertical motion
you whisper how you love me
and lick your lips unaware
with a tongue coated in the sour tang of salt and tequila

you told me you loved me
when I was sitting pretty on top of you
looking at you
biting my lower lip
with my fingertips pressed deep into your chest
and my curls toppled over to the left

I made your legs shake
and your body numb
then smiled 'cause you sound crazy

you only love me till you bust
that's not love, baby
that's lust

I know I say I want love
and get angry when you don't give it to me
but I fuel off you wanting me not loving me

this is all we know
uniting in the moonlight where we can't see
only feel
here we know each other so well

I wonder what would happen
if we carried each other to the sunlight
our tongues would be immobilized
conversation would feel foreign
our lips would be limp with insecurities

does it bother you too
that we wouldn't actually know each other at all

my lungs always freeze
as I attempt to release
the words for how I feel about you

I used to feel flustered
for not being brave

but maybe they're just protecting me
since I only feel this way
until the end of your stay

the fear
of rejection holds weight in me

I knew I should've
let you go more times
than I could count
but I tricked myself into thinking
that some of you was better
than none of you

let me narrow it
down for you
my love is stubborn right now
how can I make
this pain sound pretty

you rented a house inside my body
but only stayed between my thighs
in your favorite room
with warm walls to keep you safe from heartache
you never explored further
you never cared to see the love
that fluttered behind my rib cage
or navigate the ideas that swam in my skull
you never wanted to see
my den of emotions
or learn about my ugliest scars
you never explored further
you never cared to visit my fingertips that would've fit
perfectly with your own or smell the secrets that hid in my
hair you never wanted to hear stories
swirl seductively from my lips or learn what made me laugh
you never explored further
you simply stayed in your favorite room and wasted your
money
shame on you for not exploring my domes
but the lease must come to an end
not all houses are homes

I'm sure many can agree
but only few will admit
that life was easier before learning what life is

sometimes it saddens me that we must grow
happiness was a more frequent guest
when my legs weren't lengthy
my hair curled into spirals without spray
and ten dollars could buy me
my most miraculous dreams

when I was still small
and fueled by imagination
stories flooded from my pencil
page after page
they bloomed into life
on the lined paper before me
all I wanted was to tell a story
decorate a life with detail
I held all control
it was not until that moment of decision making
the moment I agreed on a choice of study
that my imagination went to sleep
it slept still for six years while I entertained facts
memorization and critical thinking
I lost all control
but now it is awake from its slumber
well-rested and ready to bloom again

when my mind is soft and quiet I wonder
where would I be right now
if my dreams didn't frighten me all those years ago

I put myself down before others could
as a method of protecting myself
I questioned if my presence
was being questioned
if I really belonged here

every accomplishment I collected
prior to the start of this journey
dissolved in a pool of comparison

I was no longer proud
of myself for anything

when you love what you do you should feel
electricity in your veins
here I felt unplugged

it was fascinating to feel my brain expand
with every detail I absorbed
it's a shame my passion did not

life became a colorless blur
of missing my old life,
disliking my present,
and dreaming of my future

when your heart stopped
so did mine
that's how sneaky grief can be

one afternoon you were smiling in the grass
the next you were just a memory

– December 2018

it bothered me how cold
your body became when the life left
but cherished
how warm mine felt
at the thought of you no longer suffering

– tucker

isn't it bizarre?
how they took your blonde body
and burned you into ashes
my father told me
not to think of it that way
you left your body before
you left the house that day

— cremation

the most mournful memory
was seeing your empty stocking on Christmas morning

with your wispy hair still
floating around the room like feathers
resting on the mantel gold

when our eyes witnessed the empty space
no one made a sound
it was like playing hide and seek
with a heart that would never be found

a sweet vanilla sky twinkles over the city
as I lay and watch small stars flicker like fireflies
and waltz in the clouds

I hold my gaze with the pink dust
where you journeyed home
to sleep with the other angels

as my glossy eyes stare they overflow
and I wonder
is there room for me up there too?

– heaven

emotional heartache
may sometimes surpass physical pain
so much that you might even confuse the two

in those moments be gentle with yourself
there is no timeline on healing
release little pieces of the heaviness
as you're ready

release until warmth and light
are all that exist with the memories

I left my windows opened
when I slept last night

just in case you wanted
to visit me in my dreams

phoenix

for my eighteenth birthday
I decorated my skin with a phoenix tattoo
that surfaced the entirety of my back
I let the ink sink in unapologetically
with the sting of a foreign needle

my intention was only the top left
but I knew I couldn't limit
such a bold creation
to such a small space

a phoenix rises above
it embodies feathers and claws and pupils of gems
wings so large
they could encompass an earth
a beak so sharp it could feast on anything

when it falls it forms to ashes
and reignites as a new flame stronger than its prior self

how wonderfully crazy is it
what once was spontaneous artwork soon became my greatest reminder to keep moving forward

– October 2014

Part 2: Winter/Spring 2019

I never knew how much I needed that ink
until my world started to regress

it felt the most real when I realized
I was no longer a child
playing with pastel chalk
on a lazy august afternoon

responsibility
was now mine

– reminder

I watched melted snow
freeze into icicles on the rooftops
and my breath evaporate
warm o's into the cool air

winter was here

when others inquire about my choice of study
they are always so impressed with the answer
they commend me for choosing a rewarding field
such a financially stable position and tell me I will
touch so many lives
yet every time
I envision myself in the field
despite their sweet efforts
I feel trapped and angry and overwhelmed
then wish I never
told them the answer

— how do you find your passion

permanent ink
is not permitted on our skin
until we're eighteen
in case regret were to show

yet we're expected to choose
our lifetime work
when we're seventeen
when we're still trying to grow

instead we should be
scripting lists of cities
our hearts are burning to see
swimming in the bluest oceans
mapped out so magically

– college decision

are you okay?
is the question I loathe most
I'm not okay and you know that
which is why you asked
I was fine being not okay
until you said those words
and now I feel worse
and resent you

there was a time where I'd voice my emotions
and I was told to stop complaining
my words were soaked in drama
just suck it up it will go by fast
I know it's hard but you have no choice, stop being so negative
those words tattooed themselves to my mind
my emotions were all but validated
I felt silly for seeking support

from that point on
I became the bottle no one loves
now I'm dramatic for not speaking at all
but what's the point of speaking
when no matter what my tongue spits out
it is never heard

I was once told
my personality was too lax

and maybe this wasn't the career for me

but when these little lives
tell me about their dreams
I can't help but think about myself
when they tell me
they want to open an ice cream truck
or make art all hours of the day
my voice whispers out
a resounding yes

which makes me think
that maybe I've been perfectly planted here
to be their voice of encouragement

the one I never received

why was it wholly easier
to believe the hurtful things
than the beautiful things?
I could no longer list
my loveliest qualities

my self-love became lazy
I valued myself
only as much as others did

I slowly became as empty
as the bag of milk chocolates
that lay on my nightstand

– eating my feelings

rainy daze

    the vacant library where I've been nestled for what feels like days only nonsense
        flowing from my pen
        this textbook is the last thing I want fogging my mind
        why must education be such a burden?

    sitting in seclusion, sighing with dismay my eyes slowly shift toward the window
        hidden under a blurry sheet of rain. The room is warm on my cheeks
        as the gloomy skies
        lead me into a dreamy daze of a place I'd rather be: *Newport*

    I see circles of sailboats floating atop the
        navy water like clouds as their white sails whistle in harmony
        with the seagulls' sounds

    cafes line
        the cobblestone streets with sweet scents
        of vanilla and toffee swirling out of the kitchens and into the salty air

    strolling away
        from the ice cream shop
        I see a family licking their fingers free of their treat
        and snippy students from Salve bicycling to the bookstore in a hurry
        salt-water taffy and rich fudge squares line the gift shop windows

    alongside fluffy lifeguard sweatshirts and pretty postcards waiting to be sent

    and as the day becomes later and the sun sets pink and gold
        couples stroll the brick alleyways lit by old lamp posts
        as they anticipate seafood and spritzers at
        the dockside restaurant on the water

    at the corner pub
    I see a mellow guitarist sweetly serenading his lover under twinkling lights
        that intertwine like vines in the moonlight
        she wears white lace her lips red
        and skin sun-kissed and glowing as she watches him
        from her table like a dream

    and as that final midnight chill sneaks up from the sea and swallows the flames
        from the patio candles

    I turn my gaze back to my book and to the dreary droplets of rain which have made me dream exquisitely of Newport

    – Newport, Rhode island

I began daydreaming frequently
with the newly rooted belief
that any where
was better than here:
a toxic tank of comparison
and cut-throat competition
it ate at me deeply and daily

I became so defeated
I forgot to remember the little things
that lift me up

like singing my favorite song
with the windows down or
becoming lost in the pinkest sunset

my mind had traveled elsewhere
it was distant
like a galaxy far far away from here

sitting on the shower floor with hot water
running rain down my back
into my hair
through my ears

it blocks out the head noise

my heart skipped each time my phone lit up
as if awaiting a million dollars
hoping it was you
disappointment moved in when it wasn't
so much that if it actually were to be that million
I wouldn't be fazed

it hurts me to say but
I commend you for leaving
when the fire finally died between us
that's something I was too weak
to ever do

I knew I was better off without you
but each day away hurt worse than the prior one

– codependency

I watched the candle burn
until the hot wax bath disappeared

that's how it was with us

eventually the fire died
and there was nothing left to it

everything reminds me of you
even when I blow this candle out
I think of when
you'd blow my back out

if I knew it'd be the last time
I'd lay my eyes on you
I would've held your lips a little longer
held my grip
a little stronger

when I snuck into bed
and looked at the pillow beside me
cold and untouched
I created an ocean of pity
if he can't love me
how can I love myself?

the stars saw me cry last night
but they promised
to keep my secret
if I tried to do better tomorrow

I cry and cry
and cry for you
yet I don't even know your middle name

as I search for the reason
of what it is about you

why I'm so attached
like your love is my lifeline

the answer never surfaces

the moonlight
never comes alone

it always brings emotion with it

what if our pillows could whisper? what do you think they'd say?

another night of warm rain is upon us

we miss those sunny days

we see a night sky with no moonlight, not a single twinkle in sight

only endless fields of darkness, no more passionate flickering light.

but although it has rained a lot lately, we know each droplet will grow

they will sprout those pretty pink flowers, the ones we all love and know

each flower will take its sweet time

we know they can't bloom without rain, so our pillows will quietly lay there and catch each droplet of pain

– is any one listening

if I were to write a novel
with every lie you ever told me
I'd have never ending pages
of sweet words with no spine
just a myriad of letters strung together
blankly floating in the breeze

your words were convincing
sweet but sneaky
which made believe this distorted reality was safe
knowing I was intoxicated with a toxic blend
of liquor and lust
you let me come to you
at the potential expense
of my own heartbeat

– drunk driving

every second I spent
blurry eyed behind the wheel
was a second that
a little piece of me would fade away

I'd come to you
just to come for you
and become a little emptier
while simultaneously being full
with the bliss of temporary gratification

but when it was all over
and my fingertips gripped the wheel
to drive myself away
my eyes glistened with water
and the emptiness snuck back in

each time a little more hollow
each time a little more real

I wonder when I was swallowed
this deep by the shadows
or why I thought you were powerful enough
to fill the vicious voids
sunken behind my rib cage

how did I arrive here
and how do I escape

since my absence
from your life didn't affect you
I know now
that my presence never truly mattered

do you ever feel fatigued from hearing the same broken record, the record you never asked to hear? you simply wanted a listening ear, someone to speak your mind to. so please hush, stop saying it will all get better when you have no idea
what better means

– listen don't lecture

with you gone
I had no one left to impress
forty pounds
of insecurities moved into my body
in just twelve months
I did nothing to stop it
I was letting myself go

when we were together
I felt a wholeness
like a summer garden full of florals
glistening in the wind

but once you left
I felt an emptiness
the garden became a bitter winter
where only wilted stems remain

it can be challenging to put these feelings
into words or a beautiful poem
when an anchor hugs them so tightly
weighing me down through the depths of my belly
and shyly reaching my toes
in those moments
the emptiness of an empath is unparalleled

I wonder if things
would have been different
if my obvious deterioration
was not tiptoed around like
shattered glass beneath a bare foot

the stretch marks
tell a story much greater
than too much pizza at three a.m.

they carry loss
lessons and love
all blurred into these curves
I call battle scars

Part 3: Summer 2019

the summer season in the city sprouted into the trees
with lush green leaves and flourishing flowers whose pretty pedals curled in the sunshine
it was so charming
that if you listened close enough
you could hear the fairies fluttering between them

there are days
I see myself swimming
in a pool of emotions rather than sinking, floating atop the salty water of sadness splashing cold feet in the waves overwhelmed with the joy of overcoming, but sometimes there are days
I sink so deep
that I forget how good it feels to float

– highs and lows

I came home
and cried to my father

I poured my sorrows into my hands
like they were dry plants
in desperate need of the rain

he embraced me in his arms and said nothing
it pulled the sadness from my chest like a magnet

– listening is sometimes all we need

    I've always thought happiness would show its frisky body when I followed the right path
        the path my mother told me was right and stable
        the path that would lift me up
        to the wispy pink clouds and shower me with a graceful life of love
        the path where I would be so successful and marry a beautiful Italian
        with whom I'd make chubby babies and live close to home
        the path where I'd pursue a career
        because it's safe and I'll always secure a job
        but what is the right path?
        where does happiness rest? I have yet to find it here
        how dare I follow society and let others' beliefs encompass my desires
        to conceal what I want out of this endless world
        I own a mind flickering with ideas
        for something other
        than what has been injected in me
        this is not my life
        I do not want this
        happiness must not exist

    – something deeper

I called it stress not depression
because it was more comforting to sugar coat
than surrender to vulnerability

isn't it ironic
how unhappiness can live in the happiest places

concrete jungle

    bright yellow taxis scurry to the curb honking horns in desperation
        as the scents of subway exhaust
        and candied cashews invade the air
        welcome to the city that never sleeps

        a melting pot of
        dreamers and delighted day-trippers
        shopping connoisseurs and brilliant businessmen, models and magic
        and a beautiful blend of native New Yorkers, the heart of the city bustles in
        a vibrant cloud of colors and foot traffic

        green vines coat organic sidewalk cafes with chalkboard signs
        displaying dusty letters in the sunlight while playful behaviors exquisitely evolve over fresh bread and prosecco
        meanwhile long lines for lattes wrap around the street corners as postmen wave lazy limbs advertising the newspaper

        you may hear the bells of bicycle boys
        pedaling through the pink flowers of central park as they deliver food from the pizza joint
        drop a dollar to the street show dancers whose toughness bleeds through their sleeves or sip peach bellinis with the ladies at lunch

        but Manhattan is more than the buoyant breath that circles the bright lights of times square more than the security of the

sky-high towers and more than the passionate fire
    that fuels the famous Broadway musicals
    it is a unique inclusion of heaven and hell
    a universal globe of multiformity

    – Manhattan, New York

the idea of a new opportunity excited me:
maze walking in a cultural blend of bodies
and sipping smoothies from curbside cafes
but the idea of being
buried behind a window
losing all hours of the sunlight
tore at my core

I was waiting for the last day
since the first day

this is what we call surviving
instead of living

pressure
to be successful
lived on my shoulders since I was a child
I wondered
when would it die and resurrect
as self-acceptance?

every morning
when I entered the train
I'd look around at all the others
and let my mind run wild:
their lives can't be as bad as mine I thought
she's in a cute outfit
he probably has a lunch date
that one's going shopping with her sister

I'd sit and analyze their lives as if I knew them
judge their happiness based on their appearance
then eye my boring business casual
blistered feet from ballet flats
and massage my aching shoulders
that would surrender to the floor
if I added another book to my bag

although I didn't know them
I knew they all had an advantage
they didn't have to be me

– self-pity

as I emerged from the subway steps
my eyes frosted
with the gray of the gloomy sky
speckled with a dozen clouds

it was raining so fiercely I could no longer
tell the difference on my cheeks
between those drops
and the drops from my eyelids

once I learned
that an iced latte a day
keeps the headaches away

the seven a.m. hour became the time
for coffee house blues and blonde roast

– something to look forward to

even those
who hold the world can still feel
like they hold nothing
when you are not living
in alignment

the first time I let my feelings loose
and entered a world of vulnerability
I retreated back to my nest
I've never seen you like this they'd say *you don't look like yourself*
they'd say, well what does 'myself' look like? dimpled cheeks
and smiling lips
    sun kissed skin and curvy hips-
    I guess I'm the one to blame
    they only see what I let them
    forgive me
    but bottling a broken heart
    is so much simpler than setting it free

– but smiling gets exhausting

when our resting mindset is negative
so is every wavelength of a thought that enters

since we don't attract what we want
we attract who we are

he began to call me daily
just to hear that my heart
was still fluttering like a blue butterfly
caught in an evening breeze

— dad

the goal should not be
to create new ways to escape life
rather it is to create a life
not needing to escape from

I had officially fallen to ashes
the weight became too heavy to bare
my strength evaporated
I became full of things
I always strived to be empty of
anger stress hate weight
I was officially removed from my own body

there was always something
I'd rather be doing
    always

    I needed so desperately to soften
    to shed this shell of anger

    – out of alignment

    maybe I should visit the book shop and find a love story
to indulge in
       or maybe pick petals at the floral store
       just a little something
       to invite the light back in

when did I lose myself

and no longer recognize the girl in the mirror—
the girl who loved socializing and shopping
exploring the creative arts and giggling with friends over dinner, about just how sweet life is
when did I become
the sleepy-eyed body moving through the motions
a vessel of pity
who longer wore any makeup

when did I lose myself
and how can I find her again?

it's easy to lose yourself
pouring into cups that aren't yours
you must learn
that other's wounds
are not your chores

my favorite find
of that Thursday city stroll
was the cupcake shop
on East 86th

– the little things

    the New York city pizza joint became a safe place on rainy days. I felt a cozy familiarity
        surrounded by potent bites of basil and rising dough at my nose
        the walls made me think of home and comforted me
        a tiny little parlor of red white and green with sweaty Italians shouting at each other and parmesan shakers and
        crushed red pepper flakes scattered on the condiment trays

        if time would allow I'd stay for hours nestled in the back
        salivating at saucy scents swaying to the old school tunes
        it was the perfectly painted picture of my grandmother's kitchen
        entering with an empty belly then leaving to reenter reality a little fatter
        and a little happier

if something you say is dramatic
in another person's eyes
it only means they don't understand it like you do
they don't feel the same strikes
of lightning missile
through your chest

— point of view

why is it so much easier
to write about the things that hurt me
than the things that lift me
my light shouldn't be lazy

consider this a proposal:
we are given sick days to relieve our bodies
from physical pain
to replenish the well-being that has been lost
why
are we not given sick days to relieve our minds
from mental pain
to replenish the emotional distress that has been found

physical health
should equate
mental health

this city
made me script a list
of all that I was grateful for

I saw a homeless heart curled up on the curb
with only newspaper for a home
the air was hot but his skin chilled
as I reconsidered my grievances

how dare I complain
about an envied education as another mourns
his empty belly and scarce skin
I felt foolish
immense guilt greeted me from within

endorphins
I only ran 3 miles of the 13.1 mile race
my skin was sweaty and
my untrained legs felt heavy
each lung ready to collapse inside me
I thought
do people actually run for fun?

I slipped away to the shade
to exit the race and relocate hydration
my thoughts were thanking me
I'll just train for the next one
with a secret hope the next one didn't exist

when my organs returned to rest
endorphins swam through my blood
and I felt good
really good
so good the pain seeped away from me
escaping my muscles into the heat

the urge to rip my shirt off
and pour water down my belly overcame me
I wanted to turn to my shoulder
and spit on the ground like the runners do
I felt like an Olympian
no I didn't finish but I did find pride

my gaze shifted to the sidelines
with bliss at the power of reclaiming myself
even for a simple moment

when I found my biggest fan
my father offered me a smile and said
    that's the first time I've seen you smile in a while

— when working out saved me

your beak caught my eye
as I took pruney fingers from the shower
and circled an open space on the mirror
I paused for a moment and smiled-

though you were foggy
you were still with me

you still had my back

– phoenix

Part 4: Fall 2019

convince yourself
that pain is temporary
and it suddenly becomes more tolerable

we are beings born strong
but sometimes face aches
remember this when you feel it:
pain is weakness leaving the body
let it drain
from your veins
until all you have left is your strength again

look around you

if your light is invisible
your environment needs a shift

an alteration or variation
until it glistens across oceans

I created a list of every little thing
that wounded my soul
read them aloud to the sky
and decided they would affect me no more

– progress

I woke with the moon still watching
to start the new day
more disciplined than the prior

the sweat became a release of tension
until everything in my life
shifted from black to orange

– Otf; fire five thirty

just because you house
the strength of a lion
does not mean you have to
keep fighting

don't ever forget that
hanging by a thread is still hanging

– strength

and even though I may
never visit your mind any more
I hope you know
your presence in my life holds importance
since I miss you when I'm sober

although growth showed its face compassionately
offering me fresh roots
   it still felt odd to move on without you

   but I learned that leaving is not always giving up
   it is simply recognizing that every chapter
   has an ending

   the gift is knowing
   where the last line is

why did it take my absence for you to finally realize
I was enough to fill you up

when we
no longer spoke it was the most
I ever heard from you

— we always want what we can't have

tat that on your skin
if you mean what you say

force me to believe you
with the irreversible sting of a needle
since your words thus far have proven empty

don't just sit and cry and beg me to listen

penetrate your skin for me like I would've done for you

sometimes I wonder what would be different
if we started over
would you love me more if I changed
if you changed

but the pain you caused killed all curiosity

when you finally gave me what I always wanted
I no longer wanted it any more
all desire evaporated from existence

your words didn't lift the hairs on my neck
or my soul to the sky any more
they sounded sour
like fruit that has
been basking in the air too long

at three thirteen a.m.
when the party ends
but you're still activated
on the hunt for the easiest one to break in
I am not awake

I am not available for you or your lonely soul
that thinks I will answer a thread of letters
when you're too lazy to type words
when you think "wyd"
will somehow draw me in

you'll scoff and slur at
the emptiness of no answer
then continue through your list of your options

so, at 3:13 a.m., no, I am not up
nor will I ever be for you

– lose my number

you always
made me bitter
like lemonade made
from the sourest fruit

I want someone
to make me better
like strawberries rolled
in the sweetest sugar

love is not
sitting back to see how much pain
you can take before you finally walk away
as if that somehow proves your loyalty

because all that hurt you hurdled through
won't just melt away
it will hiss in the shadows of your heart space
like unkept vines holding you hostage

until you release it
until you create a lightness
that will linger

if you play with a heart that will never fulfill you
why not seek something different
don't be swayed by weary words
be moved by energy

I've come to the conclusion
that my siblings
are my soulmates

we may have awoken
from the cosmos under different moons
but our hearts were formed in the same womb

this must be intentional-
how the fairies carried us here
to merge our journeys in this lifetime

it will take some time to remold my mindset
the one where being invisible is a feeling too familiar
I just pray my soul finds patience

— change is work

you told me I'd find a husband
only if I lost some pounds
then offer me my favorite pastry

– Italian grandmothers

I come to visit you
in your little brick house on Bradley because you light me up with your stories. you serenade my ear with your accent, a beautiful melody of culture and sacrifice when you tell me about how you fell in love or the time you learned to sew an apron

I love to hear you describe
the various colors of your fabrics
hanging thread by thread
near the sewing machine
awaiting a lucky hand to craft them

I could sit with you in the garden and watch the wet cloths
sway from the clothes pins in the dry heat of the day
or chat about your childhood under the peach tree
with cranberry juice and biscotti's
day after day after day

I like to watch the flowers bloom and the vegetable roots rise
because they remind me of you
fleeing your home for better opportunities sprouting from the dirt
into a beautiful being
and creating an abundant life worth living

your cracked hands cup my cheeks like you're cradling a baby bird with a broken wing
you tell me you're jealous of my curls even though I got them from you
and I think how lucky I am to have the honor
of being your granddaughter

– mama

you gifted me
the gold star of Italy
as a necklace to wear on my neck
I never take it off so even
when I'm not with you I'm with you

besides your family
you told me your
greatest accomplishment is your reputation

– heart of gold

my greatest childhood regret
is not learning a second language
it's fascinating to watch you
switch between tongues so smoothly

trying to please others
frequently flees from the path
of pleasing yourself
instead stay where the birds chirp
the sweet song of your soul

you tried to mold me into a mini you
I saw frustration root in your eyes
when I challenged that

you wanted so badly for me to need you
that I tried so badly to not
with every half-witted choice
my inexperienced-self committed to
I was trying to prove to myself
that I didn't need direction

how come you only tell me
you're proud of me when I get a good grade

do you not see that I can
hold the world in my hands without them

if I could enter your body for just one day I would take a cloth and wash away
    every fear in your mind

    I would open your eyes
    so you would see a hateless world
    and paint colorful pictures in your pupils of the most beautiful cities in existence

    I would force you to see all people all colors
    every language
    all choices of your children
    I would make you take a step toward the uncertain circle that you call your dreams

    I would ignite a fire under your desires so you could escape the place you hate

    I know you love me
    but do you really love me
    or do you love that you carried me

    I would make you answer that question with an honest tongue and then wipe away your disappointment

you love me
but you don't see me

you see a tiny version of the girl
who was once so easy to mold
your little girl
with wild curls
you so desperately wanted to preserve

I may still wear those
chubby cheeks and hazel eyes
but my desires differ
and deserve to be seen

I know
only one belly carried me
but two bodies created me
and three hearts raised me

even though those words may sting you to read
I hope you know I still love you loudly

my favorite memory of school
was finding your sweet love notes
hidden in my lunchbox

even on a rainy wednesday afternoon
you wanted us to know
we were loved

— mom

our twenty-four-hour trip to Chicago

    nestled in my seat buried beneath bags with enough clothing for a week

    I pressed my nose against the nippy window and settled into the twenty-two-hour

        train ride that lie ahead

    I saw a vibrant sea of colors

    a blurry blend of orange and gold tree leaves fluttering free from the branches

    and settling onto the quiet October grounds as the Amtrak rolled on

    I watched as black birds circled the sky above the endless fields we passed then swooped down

    proceeding parallel with the train

    two sisters five states and one destination: we were headed to Chicago

    although supporting our sister in the marathon and safekeeping that surprise

    was meddling with my mental

    I blocked out the head noise and sealed my eyes shut until tomorrow

when we arrived I felt it
a force that flicked life into my body
and stimulated my mind like nothing I've experienced before
an energy ensuring my presence was right
this was where I was meant to be

overwhelmed in a frenzy of fascination
we stretched our stiff muscles and set out to explore the windy city

our glossy eyes gazed the clear blue river
as choppy waves rippled beneath the tour boats and washed against the lantern-lit docks

a crisp wind swept under our hair and lead our curls into a tango
while the clock tower struck seven and we strolled along the riverwalk

towering atop us were buildings as tall as the wispy pink clouds and infinite glass windows reflecting the charm of the city
we saw painted pictures and graffitied walls as we overlooked the bridge and harkened the horns of the boats

toward the town square

millennium park was swarming with sightseers all in a dreamy architectural daze

bright green trees lined the park pathway with the plastic bodies of orange blue and purple lava rocks nestled on the brittle branches

they illuminated the way of the people

flickering like fireflies in the beams of the sunset

sometime later we boarded the train

and traveled above the city to spoil our surprise

awaiting her exit from the sky deck

hidden under sweet joy and jubilation we flung our bodies in front of her

tears of raw happiness swam to her cheeks like warm rain on an April day

together we posed with the bean and licked our fingers free

from the saucy mess of a deep-dish pie before the moon woke up to carry us home

it was now race day

the faint ring of the city bells drifted through our windows with the sunrise

we whistled for the runners while keeping close eyes
emerging from a sea of others
    her legs hustled heavily on the gravel
    our cowbells rang in sweet unison
    as we watched her wave and keep moving

    we snagged a picture with her medal
    a sour beer and a wet kiss on the cheek then headed back
to the Amtrak

    only a twenty-four-hour trip
    but a million memories that will last a lifetime

    – Chicago, Illinois

committing to that trip
reminded me of how uplifting it is
to be the reason someone smiles

– Chicago 2019

I watched my brother's life flutter into bliss when he opened his heart and spoke with an honest tongue
  it served as a reminder
  that when you flow
  you feel free

  — inspiration

often we feel frightened by solidarity
since social interaction
fuels a part of our purpose
but what if we viewed the silence
as a chance to quiet our minds for a moment
to become still like a river with no ripple

my best lines
scribble from my skin after a couple
glasses of chianti

it's where I numb away
the day unapologetically

Part 5: Spring 2020

the irony is that
we are taught we can only trust ourselves
yet sometimes
being trapped in our own mind
is the scariest place to be

how do I escape
an environment that no longer serves me any purpose

I must run from this chalky gray cloud
that loves me so much it hangs over my curly head day
after day without remorse

detox from opinions
that descend you
soak in the ones
that nourish you

what never settled
was how much of me it stole
it took all my favorite parts about myself
until I was simply
just a body not a soul

is it selfish
to want something more for myself
to bring my vivid daydreams
to physical form

flirt with ambition rather than
beg for blessings
it's much more charming

without self-reflection
there was no way to target
the parts of my life that needed
a thorough spring cleaning

when I saw the news
I felt guilty for crying to the sky
when I begged for a break
I didn't know it would bring
a global pandemic

– COVID-19

although fear grew easily during
those quiet months
don't forget the light
that came shyly with it

— rest

creative energy
began to flood the world

it overflowed in every city
country to country

there was art swirling in and among the dark
did you feel it too?

– isolation

imagine how relieving it'd be
if we could wash our minds
as easily as our hands

I wish my veins
were vanilla
so there would be nothing but sweetness
flowing through my body

sometimes I gaze at the stars
and wonder what you're doing
if you're looking at them too

but I don't miss you any more

it took me four years
to realize we were more opposite than water and oil
we were never meant to mix

I accidentally spent too much time on you
I know I can't return it
but I can learn from it

don't worry
even after everything
I still wish the best for you
your name still finds space
in my prayers

you'll try to move on
and search for me in others
but you'll never find success

because you'll realize
that my love lingers

it will nestle on your neck
like the sweetest perfume
and faintly follow you
everywhere

yesterday someone new
noticed something in me
I was worth some dinner and wine
I agreed with curiosity
except I feared I wouldn't know
how to converse in the evening
as I've only been seen at night

but to my surprise
he asked me everything
even the questions I haven't asked myself
it was like I kept a cloud of secrets in a cage
just waiting for someone to unlock it

and he was the key

— conversation

be beautifully
emotionally expressive
and whisper your heart's
song bravely

the right person will
be sweetly serenaded
the wrong one
will change the song

I learned more about him
in one evening
then I learned about you in four years

– connection

every time he spoke
it was like sitting by the fire
after too much time in the snow
I melted immediately

my body is a canvas
that I want you to paint
cover me with every color
of your wildest wounds

beg for me
like I'm the cure you've waited for
your entire life

your voice in my ears
felt like smooth jazz on a rainy night
with too much wine on my palate
dangerously cozy

if time were to stop
I'd hope the clock would halt its hands
while I'm with you

to make this moment last
to make this moment infinite

don't you dare accept being half loved
you were brought into this world whole
you deserve to be loved full

– love is a birthright

for the first time in my life
I leaned into love
I put my heart on a pedestal
the place where it always belonged

I didn't know before
but I understand now
that I must believe myself is worthy first

the riches will gently follow

I wrote my heart a love note
sealed it up tight and gave it to the wind
I thanked it for its scarlet backbone
and admired the fluttering veins
that never stopped pulsing
for anyone or anything

– strength

when I think that
it shouldn't have taken so long to appreciate myself
for all that I am
I must quiet that thought
with the outpouring gratefulness to have experienced
the journey to self-love

growth will arrive
following a challenge
just like rainbows follow the rain

if I allowed regret to swallow
a lesson learned
from a troubling experience
there wouldn't have
been blossoming

drinking was
my greatest outlet
now writing is

my heart is infused all over these pages

we woke up on the first
and decided May was the month of self-care

— sisters

vanilla oak and almond
don't those words
just work together

I sunk into
a bubble bath
wrapped in a dreamy coat of orange and oat
I soaked my limbs in soapy suds
and burned the day away

– self-care

for far too long, I'd look in the mirror and cry myself an ocean of blues. I thought my mother lied to me when she said I was gorgeous, but now I see the sun
that was absent for so many moons

when we let shoulds fog our desires
we block coulds from becoming

remember that you are the author
you always have been

imagine if time could stop but our bodies kept moving
we would be smooth
and sticky and sweet like golden honey
on a summer's day
we would live
and laugh and love
like the hours were infinite
and the boundaries did not exist
we would dance
until the moon wakes up
until the stars flicker on our skin
our lips would curve up
and our eyes would ignite at the perfect idea
of being imperfect

– before life happens

the path that should be followed
is the path our hearts lean toward
when we are too young
to make sense of it all

— listen to your heart

change used to ignite fear in me
boil my blood into a panic
now I greet it as an opportunity

trust that you
will end up exactly where you're supposed to
even if time appears to be frozen
in the pain

looking back
I realize I was too invested in my blissful past
to be present
letting go was not an option then

our minds
are one-way tickets
to our greatest desires

all you have to do
is close your eyes and trust that you'll fly

I was gifted a bouquet of creamy white petals
with drops of pastel pink and scarlet red
I inhaled deep and
curled my lips toward the sky

they smelled sweet like success

I didn't cry because
it was time to leave here
I cried because
I never thought I'd make it here

– graduation

isn't it fascinating how in its purest form
a voice is manipulated airflow?
do not hide that air
in your lungs
use your tongue to manipulate it
into meaningful words

– your voice is power

we were made with two ears
therefore
we should listen to both sides

imagine if we'd listen with our minds instead of our ears
if we'd really listen not just hear
think how beautifully
our relationships would blossom

if I tell you I feel ugly today and you say *well I think you look pretty*
I still feel ugly

if I tell you *I know how you feel*
I know what you're going through, my parents are divorced too
your parents are still getting divorced
and your heart is still bursting with sorrow
nothing changes
by attempting to relate you invalidate
by comparing your pain you disdain
by minimizing an emotion you discredit
and dismiss
the experience of another
imagine if we'd just listen not lecture
be the dry plant that needs a good watering
while others cry on our shoulders
let their pain soak into us
in a quiet cloud of breathing and being

emotions wouldn't be dismissed
to sink back beneath the skin
they would explode and evaporate to make room
for the next batch to not be buried but bloom

– counseling

holding the power of empathy
is a gift only the golden ones possess

it troubles me how
I can now hold two degrees
yet sometimes still feel like I am behind in life
the perfectionist in me
never rests

— patience

self-love
is everyday practice
be patient
but persistent

– never lose hope

when you first saw my tattoo
you cried and said
I destroyed my body
that I ruined my beautiful skin

when in reality
it saved my body
it preserved my beautiful skin

— motivation

it's never too late to start over
if you still have your breath
flowing in and away from you
there is still time

each second is a blessing

I crumbled and burned to ashes
beneath the weight of many burdens
snuggling with self-pity
moon after moon after moon

my deep desire for change was strong
but once I believed I was stronger
I rose free from the charcoal
and relit new flames of scarlet orange and gold

I flew from the ashes
like a black silhouette in the sky
for all to feast their eyes on

it was in that moment that I finally understood:

I am the phoenix.

the end.